T0064533

Keys to Living a Fulfilled Life

Keys to Living a Fulfilled Life

Concise Practical Guidance to attaining God's very best

TAIWO AYODELE

authorHOUSE®

AuthorHouse™ UK Ltd.
1663 Liberty Drive
Bloomington, IN 47403 USA
www.authorhouse.co.uk
Phone: 0800.197.4150

© 2013 by Taiwo Ayodele. All rights reserved.

No part of this book may be reproduced, stored in a retrieval system, or
transmitted by any means without the written permission of the author.

Published by AuthorHouse 12/02/2013

ISBN: 978-1-4918-8304-4 (sc)
ISBN: 978-1-4918-8303-7 (hc)
ISBN: 978-1-4918-8305-1 (e)

Any people depicted in stock imagery provided by Thinkstock are models,
and such images are being used for illustrative purposes only.
Certain stock imagery © Thinkstock.

This book is printed on acid-free paper.

Because of the dynamic nature of the Internet, any web addresses or links contained in
this book may have changed since publication and may no longer be valid. The views
expressed in this work are solely those of the author and do not necessarily reflect the
views of the publisher, and the publisher hereby disclaims any responsibility for them

Contact details: author@visionanddirections.org or info@visionanddirections.org

CONTENTS

ACKNOWLEDGEMENTS

All gratitude to God for my salvation and
for His mercies, faithfulness, loving kindness and
His guidance over the years.

I am very grateful to my **Parents, my entire family
(Dr. Abiose O, Theophilus O, Bukky I,
Dr. Dennis A, Tayo K) and to Ade & Jesse Williams**
for being such an incredible inspiration. Thanks for your
prayers, encouragements, and supports all the way.

Thanks also to IFCS Family and all who have supported
and stood in the gap. May God bless you greatly? Amen.

INTRODUCTION

This book is about living the fulfilled and successful life that God has designed for you. It is by discovering your vision, and imperatively finding out how to go about fulfilling the vision. The "How to" is the divine direction that you require to get to your destination of a fulfilled life. The discovery of your vision and gaining direction are the keys to unravelling this much desired life that glorifies God. This book further elaborates on the importance of knowing your purpose in life. Purpose is one of the most important things in life. And discovering your purpose is one of the keys to unlocking the fulfilled life that God offers you.

You are meant to be prosperous, advancing, productive in your life as Jesus emphasized in John 15:4-8 (KJV) "[4] Abide in me, and I in you. As the branch cannot bear fruit of itself, except it abide in the vine; no more can ye, except ye abide in me.[5] I am the vine, ye are the branches: He that abideth in me, and I in him, the same bringeth forth much fruit: for without me ye can do nothing.[6] If a man abide not in me, he is cast forth as a branch, and is withered; and men gather them, and cast them into the fire, and they are burned.[7] If ye abide in me, and my words abide in you, ye shall ask what ye will, and it shall be done unto you.[8] Herein is my Father glorified, that ye bear much fruit; so shall ye be my disciples. "If you allow Jesus in to your life as your personal Lord and Savior, you begin to unlock the fullness of His intentions for you. He wants you to continue to grow in Him, grow in your relationship with God and with others, grow in your Bible Study and Prayer life, grow in your walk with the Holy Spirit (Gal. 5:25), grow in: faith, wisdom, love, peace, fear of the Lord, grace, holiness, time management and expect progress in your daily life even in your career or place of employment and much more. God is interested in every aspects of your lives and expect growth in them all. In John 15:4-5, 8 (KJV), "[4] Abide in me, and I in you. As the branch cannot bear fruit of itself, except it abide in the vine; no more can ye, except ye abide in me.[5] I am the vine, ye are the branches: He that abideth in me, and I in him, the same bringeth forth much fruit: for without me ye can do nothing.[8] Herein is my Father glorified, that ye bear much fruit; so shall ye be my disciples", the scripture confirms that God is interested in a life that is prosperous, fulfilled, wealthy, creative, and productive as these glorify Him. Your fulfilment in life gives glory, praise, exaltation, dignity and honour to God.

You need to improve your life, be a better parent, friend, better communicator, better wife, better husband, better employer, exceptional employee, exceptional boss, exceptional student, exceptional leader and an exceptional child of God. You are created to be great, have a prosperous life and also enjoy your life (Jer. 29:11, John 10:10) because you are fearfully and wonderfully made (Ps. 139:14). God wants you to be more like Him (Eph. 5:1, Heb. 12:2).

Friend, even if you are living your fulfilled life now, it is imperative that you must not be torpid. 'God's is interested in your increase, advancement, progress, growth—John 15:4-8. Keep moving forward in your career, studies, relationship, marriage and much more as He commanded the Israelites—Exo. 14:14-15 (KJV) "14 The LORD shall fight for you, and ye shall hold your peace.15 And the LORD said unto Moses, Wherefore criest thou unto me? speak unto the children of Israel, that they go forward:" Friend, start improving your life and aspire to make progress according to the will of God.

This book further explains the importance of knowing God, importance of forgiving people, knowing the ways of God—How He works, understanding your purpose, and getting to know how to fulfil your purpose—direction from God. Psalm 32:8 (NKJV) "I will instruct you and teach you in the way you should go; I will guide you with My eye." Living a purpose driven life will eradicate a life of toiling, struggling, trial and error, untimely death. Purpose guarantees your reason for existence.

With each page, you are stepping intently into the life God designed you for and lovingly desires for you.

CHAPTER ONE

Why I write This Book

The time that we are in is very crucial and it seems most Christians do not realize the season and importance of the time that we are in right now. Unlike Men of Issachar—*"from Issachar, men who understood the times and knew what Israel should do—200 chiefs, with all their relatives under their command"* (1 Chron. 12:32 NIV). These men understood their duties, calling, purpose, commitment, career, obligations, business, job, vision and what they ought to do at every point in time. They were never once confused about their vision, calling, best life, fulfilled life that has been offered to them. In fact they had directions, control, dominion, governance and took charge of their success, breakthroughs, having a deep understanding, keen awareness and discernment. During King David's time, they also understood:

- It was a crucial time because it was destined that David should be king over all Israel. The "times"— They understood the periods and seasons when things usually took place. They also knew when it would be time for particular event to take place

- They were able to interpret God's written word by recognizing the significance of past events and applying the lessons to the present and the future

- The men of Issachar understood what God was about to do, and was a great help in establishing David's rule as David needed such men during this crucial time in Israel

- The men of Issachar was able to guide and advise David in making sure he did not fail to accomplish the task of integrating the entire kingdom under his reign.

God wants us to understand the vision and purpose why He created us—to praise Him (Ps. 22:3), also to enjoy the best life He destined us for (John 10:10b). It is time for us to enjoy a life of fulfilment as this book explore the principles of living a fulfilled life—Best Life offered to us. Now is the time to enjoy the best in God.

CHAPTER TWO

Fulfilled Life

*I came that they may have and enjoy life, and have it in
abundance (to the full, till it [b] overflows)*
John 10:10b (AMP)

It is obvious that God has a good intention for you and
affirming this from Jesus himself put a smile on our
faces. God created us in His image to live a fulfilled life,
an unlimited life—with excellent career, marital, academic,
financial breakthroughs, success, divine health, marital
stability, consistent spiritual growth, structured and well
established life and much more.

*God made you on purpose for a purpose. He has a job for
you that no one else can do as well as you. Out of billions of
applicants, you are the most qualified—***John Mason**

To attain this unlimited and fulfilled life, you need to
aspire to be like Him—"*Therefore be imitators of God
[copy Him and follow His example], as well-beloved children*

[imitate their father]" Eph. 5:1(AMP). Friends, do not be like someone else as some desire to be like a celebrity or an individual in the way they dress, look, speak, walk, and even in the way they live. And for some, they tend to follow the trend of fashion, technologies, they want to go where the crowd is going, live extravagantly the way they see others live. When you try to be like someone else that you are not, the best you can ever be is second best. Do realize now that people can deceive you with their lifestyle, their attitudes, their expensive cars but it may surprise you that they are living on credit cards or even on debts. What a life! It is high time you take your eyes off others and focus on God. God will always keep you on track and for you to become the successful, fulfilled person He intended you to be. Be whom He has created you to be and use the resources he has given you.

Read about the story of a middle-aged woman who had a heart attack and was rushed to the emergency room. On the operating table, she had a near-death experience. This woman met God during her stay in the hospital and she asked God if this was the end of her life and He said, "No, you have another forty-three years, two months and eight days to live." Upon recovery, she decided to stay in the hospital and have a face-lift, liposuction, a tummy tuck, the whole works. She even had someone come in and change her hair color, figuring that since she had so much life remaining, she might as well make the most of it.

She was discharged after the final procedure, however, while crossing the street outside, she was killed by a speeding ambulance. Arriving in God's presence, she fumed, "I thought you said I had another forty-plus years." He replied, "I did not recognize you." Be yourself. Think about that. Do not imitate people. The Psalmist says "*I will praise thee; for I am fearfully and wonderfully made: marvellous are thy works; and that my soul knoweth right well.*" Ps. 139:14 (KJV). Why wouldn't you be who God has created you to be? Why do you have to change any part of your body or try to be someone you are not supposed to be or engage in things you are not meant to be involved with? Living such a life will limit the unlimited and fulfilled life that God intended for your life. For you to live the unlimited life offered to you, you have got to be an imitator of God in your action, in attitudes, in all areas of your life even in your work place, academic environment, with friends and family, with neighbors and live in peace with everyone.

CHAPTER THREE

Live Above Your Past

18 "Forget the former things;
do not dwell on the past.
19 See, I am doing a new thing!
Now it springs up; do you not perceive it?
I am making a way in the wilderness
and streams in the wasteland—Isa. 43:18-18 (NIV)

There is nothing wrong in having unpleasant memories, but when we worry about what has already passed, we fall out of fellowship with God. Many today are harboring hurt, hatred, resentment, malice, unforgiveness, and host of unresolved issues that have happened to them in the past either in previous relationships, marriages, in school, university, in the family, with friends or at place of work. One should realize that the most detrimental thing that we do to harm our spiritual relationship and walk with God is to dwell on the past. We think about what happened minutes, hours, days, months, or even years that have already passed and we allow that to shape our thought life, our perception and the way we relate to others.

Do you still remember the horrible experiences of early age childhood, poverty experience or lack, limited education, guilt over mistakes made, opportunities missed, low self-esteem, loss of parents when growing up, death of loved ones, failed exams, unsuccessful marital life, broken promises, lack of confidence due to ailment, loneness, insecurity due to emotional instability, divorce parental experiences and the list goes on. It is crucial to know and to remember that your past is over.

What about memories of stigma of questionable events of the past? You are not alone, Jesus passed through such stigma and societal label. In Mat. 1:18-23 (AMP) "*[18] Now the birth of Jesus Christ took place under these circumstances: When His mother Mary had been promised in marriage to Joseph, before they came together, she was found to be pregnant [through the power] of the Holy Spirit.*

[19] And her [promised] husband Joseph, being a just and upright man and not willing to expose her publicly and to shame and

disgrace her, decided to repudiate and dismiss (divorce) her quietly and secretly.

20 But as he was thinking this over, behold, an angel of the Lord appeared to him in a dream, saying, Joseph, descendant of David, do not be afraid to take Mary [as] your wife, for that which is conceived in her is of (from, out of) the Holy Spirit.

21 She will bear a Son, and you shall call His name Jesus [the Greek form of the Hebrew Joshua, which means Savior], for He will save His people from their sins [that is, prevent them from [a] failing and missing the true end and scope of life, which is God].

22 All this took place that it might be fulfilled which the Lord had spoken through the prophet,

23 Behold, the virgin shall become pregnant and give birth to a Son, and they shall call His name Emmanuel—which, when translated, means, God with us."

The scriptures above explained that Joseph had no sexual relationship with Mary the mother of Jesus. Mary conceived before she married Joseph and what we understand is that it is only God that knew that Mary was a virgin as the scripture elaborated. You can imagine what went through the mind of Joseph—verses 19-20: *And her [promised] husband Joseph, being a just and upright man and not willing to expose her publicly and to shame and disgrace her, decided to repudiate and dismiss (divorce) her quietly and secretly, 20, But as he was thinking this over, behold, an angel of the Lord appeared to him in a dream, saying, Joseph, descendant of David, do not be afraid to take Mary [as] your wife, for that which is conceived in her is of (from, out of) the Holy Spirit.* No male who has not had any contact with his wife would believe or like to understand the situation of Mary to the extent that even Joseph was thinking of repudiating and dismissing Mary until he had a personal encounter with God that changed his perception and believed the Holy Spirit. Imagine thousands of people mocked, gossiped and sneered at Joseph for accepting Mary. This is the sort of controversial stigma that Jesus went through.

Jesus was faced with series of these questionable events as he was growing up but he learnt to ignore such remarks, and it was never written that Jesus allowed this stigma to affect His vision on earth. He has never mentioned or discussed these slanderous remarks or stigma. Unlike some of us, we make the stigma of questionable events of the past the talk of the town, a major issue and this can in turn affect your new relationships, marriage, your career, family and friends; and this can strain or put pressure on other people in your life or around you. Jesus did not allow this stigma to be an issue at all. This issue was never allowed to affect His vision and purpose why He came—to seek and to safe those who are lost. He was doing good, healing the sick, raising the dead, preaching every day. He was not accusing His mother or father of wrongdoing because He knew the truth, knew who He was. He did not allow the opinion of others to affect Him. He chose to focus on His mission and there is no place in the scripture that stated that Jesus discussed or brought up His background.

It is high time we move forward. Stop focusing on your yesterday or events that you cannot describe or explain why it happened to you. Stop pointing accusing finger at people, family, friend, workplaces, organizations, the country or the economy and stop blaming others for past mistakes. Understand that everyone has limitations. Do what Jesus did, He focused on His vision and purpose why He came (Luke 4:43, Luke 19:10), He did not focus on His background or on the things of the past but rather focused on the future and His mission here on earth. That is one of the secrets of living a fulfilled life.

The curious paradox is that when I accept myself just as I am, then I can change—Carl Rogers

Rise above your past, rise above stigma of questionable events of the past. Do what Jesus and Paul did. Paul also demonstrated to us how to handle life situations and displayed practical ways to face the future and that was one of his secrets of fulfilment in life. Phil. 3:13-14 *"Brethren, I count not myself to have apprehended: but this one thing I do, forgetting those things which are behind, and reaching forth unto those things which are before, [14] I press toward the mark for the prize of the high calling of God in Christ Jesus."* You too should learn to forgive people, forget negative histories, negative memories of the past and learn to look ahead to the new future that God has promised—an abundant life, successful and fulfilled life—John 10:10b.

CHAPTER FOUR

Forgiveness: Key to Unlocking Fulfillment and Fruitfulness

31 Let all bitterness, and wrath, and anger, and clamour, and evil speaking, be put away from you, with all malice:

32 And be ye kind one to another, tender-hearted, forgiving one another, even as God for Christ's sake hath forgiven you—Eph. 4:30-31

13 Bear with each other and forgive one another if any of you has a grievance against someone. Forgive as the Lord forgave you—Col. 3:13

Human behavior suggests that people are "hard-wired" to retaliate when they have been hurt by another person. Our pride or self-esteem is injured. Our expectations or dreams are disappointed. We lose something very valuable to us. We want recompense for the damages.

But there are other resistances which block our motivation to forgive. Automatic thoughts or beliefs impede us from forgiving others. We tell ourselves, "I won't forgive because he/she never accepts responsibility for what he/she does" or "I would be a hypocrite if I forgave because I do not feel like forgiving" or "Forgiving is only for weak people".

*Explanations for behavior can also get in the way. When someone hurts us or lets us down we tend to assign internal causes for behavior to others. We argue that it is based personality or character traits. We tell ourselves, "he's just so forgetful or careless" or "she doesn't appreciate me" or "she did that purposefully". We judge them harshly—***Lynette Hoy***

What about feeling of hurt, broken relationships, unresolved conflicts, guilt, deception, bitterness, disappointments, unmet expectations, long standing issues, lack of appreciation, bleeding heart which could be as a result of things that happened to you either with friends, family, colleagues, with your boss, in relationships hoping to lead to marriage but does not and much more. Friends, living a life of unforgiveness births grudge, retaliation, unsettled mind and a deep seated grudge in your life will eat away your peace of mind.

When you live a life of unforgiveness, revenge naturally follows. Revenge is deceptive. It looks sweet, but it is truly bitter. It is manlike to punish but Godlike to forgive. Living a life of unforgiveness is like leaving the parking brake on when you drive your car: It drags! It causes you to slow down and lose your momentum—**John Mason**

If you do not forgive people, such life will be in a cycle of revenge, retaliations, resentment, bitterness, malice and much more. Is that what you want your life to be like? Of Couse not. One of the keys to unlocking the fulfilled life that God has destined for you is to forgive people, everyone that might have offended you even daily. Forgiveness is a key to having peace and living in peace with all men— Heb. 12:14 *"⁴ Pursue peace with all people, and holiness, without which no one will see the Lord." Make every effort to live in peace with everyone and be holy—(NIV). Work at getting along with each other and with God. Otherwise you'll never get so much as a glimpse of God—(MSG).* Forgiveness creates peace, freedom and releases you. Paul the apostle understood the principles and benefits of forgiveness— Phil. 3:12-14 *"¹² Not that I have already attained, or am already perfected; but I press on, that I may lay hold of that for which Christ Jesus has also laid hold of me. ¹³ Brethren, I do not count myself to have apprehended; but one thing I do,* **forgetting those things which are behind and reaching forward to those things which are ahead,** [14] *I press toward the goal for the prize of the upward call of God in Christ Jesus.* Paul learnt and understood that dwelling on negative memories of the past and unforgiveness will hinder him from making accurate judgment of things, will make him feel angered, bitter towards people or things, feel a sense of revenge or retaliation, resentment, and will miss the opportunities ahead of him in the future. He chose God's way of forgiveness Mat. 6:14—[14] *"For if you forgive men their trespasses, your heavenly Father will also forgive you.* [15] *But if you do not forgive men their trespasses, neither will your Father forgive your trespasses."* Forgive yourself of mistakes, errors, forgive everyone that offended you as God also will forgive you too.

No one can be wrong with man and be right with God
—Harry Emerson

Stop arguing, stop claiming rights, you can be wrong in the middle of being right when you do not forgive someone. You cannot claim that you cannot forgive and be right with God. NO. That is not possible. Mat. 6:14 explains it all. If you do not forgive people, your heavenly Father will not forgive you either. When Paul did, he was able to make right judgment of things and fulfil his career. He understood that if the creator of the universe did not forgive you, no matter what you do on earth, no matter your intelligence, such a life will not be fulfilled in Him. Start putting things right in your life. Release your past for the future to be fulfilled.

> *30 And do not grieve the Holy Spirit of God, by whom you were sealed for the day of redemption. 31 Let all bitterness, wrath, anger, clamor, and evil speaking be put away from you, with all malice. 32 And be kind to one another, tenderhearted, forgiving one another, even as God in Christ forgave you.*
> —Eph. 3:30-32

Seven Consequences of Unforgiveness

1. **Not forgiving opens doors for Satan to operate:** 2 Cor. 2:10-11 (MSG) *"So if you forgive him, I forgive him. Don't think I'm carrying around a list of personal grudges. The fact is that I'm joining in with your forgiveness, as Christ is with us, guiding us. After all, we don't want to unwittingly give Satan an opening*

for yet more mischief—we're not oblivious to his sly ways!" Not forgiving opens the door for the enemy to work in your life, forgiving will block and stop the enemy from taking advantages of us. God wants us to forgive "lest Satan should take advantage of us" (2 Corinthians 2:11). If you do not forgive, you open the door for the enemies to come in. Learn to forgive and all doors of mischievousness will be closed and you will have your life back on tract.

2. **It hinders your prayers from being answered:** Mark 11:25 (AMP) *"25 And whenever you stand praying, if you have anything against anyone, forgive him and [a]let it drop (leave it, let it go), in order that your Father Who is in heaven may also forgive you your [own] failings and shortcomings and let them drop."* That suggests that such prayers will be on hold, such blessing will be on hold until you let go. Your forgiveness will allow God to reach you, bless you and your prayers will be answered. "Isa. 1:19—*If you are willing and obedient, You shall eat the good of the land;"* Do your best to forgive first. That now means you have reached out for Him and He can then reach out to help you or forgive you. That way,

the devil can never accuse God of injustice. Friend, do you see how we do put God into such difficult situations and put blame on Him at all times? We have got to change our perception and be obedient to Him. That way, we won't give the devil an opportunity to accuse us or accuse God of wrong doing. We can then live the Christ-like life easily.

3. **It contaminates who you are:** James 3:11 *"¹¹ Does a spring send forth fresh water and bitter from the same opening?* If you are unforgiving, your perception of things or people will be different and your reactions to them will be different. Your desires and actions are polluted and such individuals may be speaking out of anger, rage, malice, retaliation or revenge because their heart is already polluted. That is why the scripture in Prov. 4:23 *"Keep your heart with all diligence, for out of it spring the issues of life."* This scripture encourages us to forgive and guard our hearts.

4. **It paves way for revenge: Prov.** 24:29: *"Do not say, "I will do to him just as he has done to me; I will render to the man according to his work."* When you do not

forgive, it causes one to entertain thoughts of revenge or fight back.

5. **It can lead to a life of torment:** Mat. 18:33-35 *"Should you not also have had compassion on your fellow servant, just as I had pity on you?'* ³⁴ *And his master was angry, and delivered him to the torturers until he should pay all that was due to him.* ³⁵ *"So My heavenly Father also will do to you if each of you, from his heart, does not forgive his brother his trespasses."* Not forgiving can lead to emotional instability, emotional torture, making irrational decisions, and excruciating actions or experience. This can also be personal torture too. Why will you be torturing yourself when you can let go and forgive? Do not torture yourself anymore. Forgiveness alleviates you from such a life.

6. **Not forgiving means you are walking in darkness:** 1 John 2:11 *"¹¹ But he who hates his brother is in darkness and walks in darkness, and does not know where he is going, because the darkness has blinded his eyes."* It is a life full of delusion, confusion, and lack of direction. One of the keys to fulfilment in life

is to get directions from God. But a life that is not forgiving does not have access to divine directions from God. The best way is to always forgive so that you can have divine access to your heavenly Father.

7. **It means you will not be forgiven by God:** Mat. 6:15 *"But if you do not forgive men their trespasses, neither will your Father forgive your trespasses."* So, what is the point living life without the support, assurance, and guidance from the Creator? That means such a life is disconnected, disassociated, prone to derailment, prone to mistakes and much more because the source of power, the leader and the Author of such life does not allow such life. When you do not forgive, it means that you do not approve of God intervening in your life and situations. In Rev. 3:20—*20 Behold, I stand at the door and knock. If anyone hears My voice and opens the door, I will come in to him and dine with him, and he with Me.* God will not force Himself or His decisions on you, you decide if you want to forgive and He shall give the enablement to do so. But when you refuse to forgive, you do not give Him permission to help you, you do not give Him permission to make His

enabling power that can heal your heart, heal your wounds, make you forgive and help you forget the past available to you. God wants us to allow Him to intervene in all areas of our lives and one way to allow God is to FORGIVE. Forgive yourself, and forgive people that offended you.

Being aware of these seven consequences will be useful for releasing God's divine directions, accessing His throne of grace, having the assurance of fulfilment that is very vital and essential to the fulfilled life He has made available to us.

CHAPTER FIVE

Knowing God's Master Plan For Your Life

Are you now ready for the best life, career, relationship, finances that you have been promised? Do you want to fulfill your days? Know that you can fulfill your days and live a quality life here on earth. But when you notice unproductiveness, you need to excavate it to find out why. It is the right thing to re-evaluate your life, to find out what went wrong and what is causing the unproductiveness.

Life is a seed, life is also about sowing and reaping. There will never be a day in your life that you will not sow and likewise there will never be a day in your life that you will not harvest. The scripture says *"While the earth remaineth, seedtime and harvest, and cold and heat, and summer and winter, and day and night shall not cease"*—Gen. 8:22. So, whatever you sow is your seed, whatever you reap is your harvest. Sowing and reaping is like breathing in and breathing out. Understanding the concept of sowing and reaping is the foundation of realising how you can live a successful life that is stress free. Now that you realised that your life is so important and it is a gift from God, you must receive Christ into your life—John 3:16, John 17:3. You need to invest time in knowing the purpose of God for your life in order to live your life to the best.

You will also realise that one of the most important thing in life is '**purpose**'. God is more concerned about His purpose for your life. Myles Munroe explained that *"The most tragic thing in life is not death but it is a life without a purpose—* being in life without knowing why?" Why are you in this world? What is your reason for existence? What are you meant to be doing? Prov. 19:21—*"many plans are in a man's mind, but it is the Lord's purpose for him that will stand".* God wants us to align our plan with His plan. He wants us to submit our ideas, intentions, creativities, thoughts and align them with His purpose—His original reason why we are created. If the plans or thoughts or intentions or ideas are inline, then God's plan for our life will stand. Purpose is more important to God and His desires are for us to discover them and live a purpose driven life. Purpose is the original intention of God for you, his original reason why

He created you, original reason for your existence on earth. Discovering this is good news.

Otherwise, many are just living their lives without knowing God's purpose and also without a sense of directions. This is why many are unproductive and life seems stressful, painful, seems to be challenging and difficult. This is why this book is relevant to your life and will liberate you from all ignorance and lies of the evil one. God has created you to be successful and fruitful (Gen. 1:28). Fruitfulness is God's commands right from creation. Fruitfulness means success, abundance, prosperity, richness, fertility. In John 15:8 *"When you bear (produce) much fruit, My Father is honored and glorified, and you show and prove yourselves to be true followers of Mine"*, this indicated that God wants His disciples to bear fruits (increase, live a good life, be rich, be in good health, win souls, so that God will be glorified. God is not glorified in you being a failure, mediocre, unproductive, unsuccessful, and unhappy. That is never God's intention. God's will for your life is to be fruitful, productive, successful, increase, to have a peaceful and healthy relationship, peaceful and enjoyable married life, good career, happy family, abundance life, rich and quality life. His intentions are further explained here:

- Gen. 1:26,28, John 10:10
- Jer. 29:11, John 17:3,5-6
- John 3:16, Luke 4:43 and much more

So, having discovered what you are here on earth for through a discovery of purpose, the next thing is to know how to accomplish the task you have been sent to perform, that is the pursuit of purpose. This is where divine guidance comes in. Now, realising that God created you to perform a specific task, He should then be allowed to show you how to do it. A manufacturer is the only one that knows best what the product is designed for and knows the functionalities and capabilities and that is why every product comes with manufacturer's manual. This could explain how best to use such a product.

Let's look at people that knew God's purpose and were successful. Jeremiah had his purpose of existence revealed even when he was in the womb (Jer. 1:5), Moses (Exo. 33:12-14) knew God's purpose and he knew God's ways, Simon Peter (Luke 5:5) knew Jesus's purpose for his life by obeying, submitting to His instructions and his life and the lives of other fishermen around him never remain the same. They were successful and they made it in life. If you want your life to be improved and live the best life that God has promised you daily with joy, peace, rest roundabout, you have got to change your attitude towards God, toward the way you live your life, be willing to follow God and obey all His instructions. Being successful is not about the people you know, is not about who knows you, is not about the Government that is in power, is not about how intelligent you are. No. It is in the hands of God—Ps. 31:15 "*My times are in thy hand: deliver me from the hand of mine enemies, and from them that persecute me*". But you have got to change your attitude towards God for things to begin to work in your life. Chapter six explains the in depth secrets of experiencing God, having the knowledge of God and the benefits so that you can enjoy the long lasting life He is offering you today.

CHAPTER SIX

Knowing God's Way

Many are conversant with God's promises but only few are familiar with His ways. God's ways are different from our ways as the scripture says—Isa. 55:8-9 "For my thoughts are not your thoughts, Nor are your ways My ways, says the Lord, For as the heavens are higher than the earth, So are My ways higher your ways, And My Thoughts than your thoughts". Man's ways are usually contrary to God's. Matthew 16:21-24—"From that time forth began Jesus to shew unto his disciples, how that he must go unto Jerusalem, and suffer many things of the elders and chief priests and scribes, and be killed, and be raised again the third day. Then Peter took him, and began to rebuke him, saying, Be it far from thee, Lord: this shall not be unto thee. But he turned, and said unto Peter, Get thee behind me, Satan: thou art an offence unto me: for thou savourest not the things that be of God, but those that be of men. Then said Jesus unto his disciples, If any man will come after me, let him deny himself, and take up his cross, and follow me". Peter reasoned that Jesus should not have to die. Peter could not see the whole picture as he had his own idea how Jesus should react, or how the plan should work out. He did not see that God was redeeming the world through the death of Jesus. He did not know that the plan and purpose of Jesus was to die for us so as to save us from our sins. Imagine the tragedy if Peter had his way. We would not have had our redemption through the blood of Jesus even salvation of soul. Rationalizing often sets us against God. Maybe salvation would not have been possible but thanks to God whose ways and thoughts are the best.

God made known His ways to Moses—Ps. 103:7 *"He made known his ways unto Moses, his acts unto the children of Israel"*. He showed Moses how it went about His work, how His new way of doing things, His approach, and manner is different from ours and this is revealed to Moses. In other words, Moses understood God's way, acquainted and experienced God's methods. In fact, he knew God's purposes, plans and directions for the Israelites. So, God's acts, purpose, plans were known by the children of Israel. This means that the children of Israel knew the miracles, wonders that God performed, they saw the ten plagues (Exo. 7-11). The water from the rock (Exo. 17:6), the division of the red sea (Exo. 14:21), Manna from Heaven

(Exo. 16:35) and during the time of the apostles, people saw the feeding of the five thousand (John 6:9-12), the blind receiving sight, the lame walking, deaf hearing and the dead raised (Mat. 11:5). All these are all God's acts, plans, and His doings. The Israelites knew His acts (His doings, acquainted with His promises) as we might have, or experienced or heard but the majority did not know His ways.

Many of us are familiar with God's promises but only a few knows God's way. Friend, peradventure God might have protected you from danger, healed you of diseases, promoted you at your place of work, allowed you to have the excellent life or be the best in what you do, all these are His doings, plans, promises for your life and without knowing him—having an intimate knowledge of God, truth, revelation of Him it means that your knowledge of Him is shallow and superficial. God's intention is that you should know Him *"And this is eternal life: [it means] to know (to perceive, recognize, become acquainted with, and understand) You, the only true and real God, and [likewise] to know Him, Jesus [as the] Christ (the Anointed One, the Messiah), Whom You have sent—John 17:3 (AMP)"*. Jesus also explained that eternal life is knowing God (John 17:3) while Heb.8:11 *"And they shall not teach every man his neighbour, and every man his brother, saying, Know the Lord: for all shall know me, from the least to the greatest"*.

Today, do you want to know God intimately, do you want to know God's will for your life, the best career you are meant to be in, the future partner that God has provided for you, the city that God has destined you to be, the opportunities that you suppose to have, the free things that God has in store for you—1 Cor. 2:12 *"Now we have received, not the spirit of the world, but the spirit which is of God; that we might know the things that are freely given to us of God"*. God created you to live a good life, in fact in John 10:10b, He gave you an abundance life, everlasting life, a life that is full of God's Glory, Peace, Joy in the Holy Ghost. This is the life He has created you to live. If you are ready and willing to enjoy the best in this planet earth, this book is for you as a revelation from God to you. Hosea 4:6 *"My people are destroyed for lack of knowledge: because thou hast rejected knowledge . . . ."*. Today, do not reject knowledge, do not ignore God, do not procrastinate receiving God into your life. Remember, He is your creator; He knew you right from the womb (Jer. 1:5). So, He knew the best job you should be doing here on earth, He knew how you should live a life without struggle, oppression, depression, opposition, limitations, lack etc. He is the architect of this earth. An architect instructs or guides you into knowing the property details in comparison to an estate agent because the architect has in-depth knowledge of the property. Many have mortgaged their lives into the hand of agents rather than the architect of their soul that knows everything about them and can also provide solutions to their lives. Friends, let's wake up, let's rise up to the new life that God has for us—a Glorious life (Isa. 60:1).

Life examples in the scriptures: Abraham knew God's way of doing things and he interceded for Sodom standing on God's righteousness (Gen. 18:23-33), Moses understood God's ways (Ps. 103:7) and the benefits of knowing God and His ways is exemplified in the life of Moses— Exo. 33:17 "17 And the Lord said to Moses, I will do this thing also that you have asked, for you have found favor, loving-kindness, and mercy in My sight and I know you personally and by name." If you allow God into your life today also, you too will have whatever you asked God for with favor, loving-kindness, mercy and special privilege of being identified with Him (To be call the sons of God). He is an awesome God. David refused to offer burnt offering that cost him nothing (1 Chron. 21:24) because he knew God's ways. So, to know God's way is to know Him personally. Having a personal relationship with Him, accept Jesus into your life as your personal Lord and saviour—John 3:3-5, and 16.

Phil. 3:10-11 *"I gave up all that inferior stuff so I could know Christ personally, experience his resurrection power, be a partner in his suffering, and go all the way with him to death itself. If there was any way to get in on the resurrection from the dead, I wanted to do it"*. Knowing God means "Giving up worldliness, giving up sins—anger, rage, bitterness, resentment, lies, pornography, sex before marriage, clubbing, all uncleanliness, all manifest of the flesh (Gal. 5:19-21), all things that are not in Christ Jesus, it is time to give them up so that you can have the life of Christ in you (Eph. 5:1).

If you have made up your mind just as Paul the apostle did, do pray this prayer:

"Lord Jesus, I come to your presence today to ask for forgiveness of my sins . . . (State and confess the sin, be specific), I want you to have mercy on me.

I have decided to part ways with my past, let my past be deadened in Jesus name. Amen. I am delivered from the powers of darkness into your kingdom today. I am redeemed by the blood of Jesus, I accept Jesus as my personal Lord and Saviour, lead and take full control of my life from now on in Jesus name. Amen"

Congratulations! You are now enrolled in the Kingdom of God. Your new and successful life has begun. Welcome to the kingdom of God where God reigns. In the next chapter, we shall be learning benefits of knowing God and how to continue to know Him and grow in our walk with Him.

CHAPTER SEVEN

Benefits of Knowing God Personally

There are amazing benefits of knowing God, but such benefits are there only if we know God as He reveals Himself to us and it is not enough to be more spiritual, we must be attuned to God as we get to learn about Him and who we are in Him. Paul explained this explicitly in Eph. 1:17-19 "*[For I always pray to] the God of our Lord Jesus Christ, the Father of glory, that He may grant you a spirit of wisdom and revelation [of insight into mysteries and secrets] in the [deep and intimate] knowledge of Him, ¹⁸ By having the eyes of your heart flooded with light, so that you can know and understand the hope to which He has called you, and how rich is His glorious inheritance in the saints (His set-apart ones), ¹⁹ And [so that you can know and understand] what is the immeasurable and unlimited and surpassing greatness of His power in and for us who believe, as demonstrated in the working of His mighty strength*". As you have a deep and intimate relationship with God you will receive "Enlightened heart, Hope, Riches of His Glorious inheritance, and Power".

Enlightened Heart

The heart is the core of man's self. The heart is so strong and powerful, and that is why the devil keeps fighting you in your mind. Everything that makes life worth living flows from the heart—Love, Success, Vision, Purpose, Excellence, Prosperity, Godly relationships, Good Career etc. If you think in your heart that you can achieve greatness, be a company director, own a business, a pilot, a millionaire—Yes, you can with the work and by the Grace of God. Prov. 23:7a *"For as he thinks in his heart, so he is"*, (Prov. 23:7a, Phil. 4:13). God promises to grant us our heart desires—Ps. 37:4. One of strategies of the devil is to break our hearts through jealousy, pettiness, unforgiveness, malice, strife, confusion, gossip, and blaming others for our mistakes and poisoning our thought life. The psalmist's heart was broken by sin—Ps. 51:1-11 but the good news is that, if we exercise true confession (acknowledging that you did wrong rather than blaming others or the situation), you will experience a new transformation (Rom. 12:1-2) and God will create in you a new heart and renew a right spirit within you. You heart will be flooded with light—illuminations, directions, solutions. God blessed us with this benefit of enlightened heart so that we can have access to the wondrous things that God has in store for us—Ps. 119:18 *"Open my eyes, that I may see Wondrous things from Your law"*. In addition, now that your heart is enlightened (not blinded), the deceiver cannot deceive you anymore, you can get rid of the doubt, unstable mind, defeat any form of enticement of the devil. This is one of the benefits of knowing God personally.

Hope

God wants you to see exactly what He has created you to achieve, attain, accomplish in life. Do you know exactly why you are on this earth for? Do you know what you should be doing, do you know the career you should be in, the future partner you should marry, your destiny and how to achieve them. His 'HOPE' is His plans for your life as revealed in Jer. 29: 11 *"For I know the thoughts that I think toward you, saith theLORD, thoughts of peace, and not of evil, to give you an expected end"* and John 10:10b *"I am come that they might have life, and that they might have it more abundantly"*. Also, understanding His Purpose and calling and how they are aligned to the advancement of His Kingdom is very important. One of the benefits of having deep intimate relationship with God is that He will reveal His Purpose here on earth to you but you need to get directions through the help of the Holy Spirit and by studying the word of God on how you can use the revealed purpose and calling for God's glory. King David used his position and calling for God's glory, King Solomon did same, Luke (Medical Doctor—Col. 4:14) use his career for God's purpose, Mathew (Tax Collector—Mat. 9:9-10) did, Paul (was a Tentmaker—Acts 18:3, Prosecutor—Acts 9:4) then became a Preacher—Gal. 1:1, 16 (after he gave his life to Christ) used his career for God's glory. Whatever position you find yourself, use it for God's glory and you will never regret it. The hope of our calling is also the absolute certainty of our heavenly destiny and includes all that awaits the saints at the return of the Lord Jesus.

The riches of the glory of his inheritance in the saints

This is another great benefit of having an intimate relationship with God. You will enjoy the abundance of God's splendid possessions in Christ. God himself took charge of His people. The saints are His inheritance first of all and He considers them as a treasure of incomparable worth! In Ephesians 1:14 Paul spoke of our inheritance, but here seems to speak of God's inheritance in believers. As saints, we are God's inheritance, His treasure, His prize! Our riches are in God and He takes charge of His saints (Deu. 32:9). Also, the other view is that the inheritance means all that we will inherit in Christ and is only guaranteed through the Holy Spirit—Eph. 1:14 *"That [Spirit] is the guarantee of our inheritance [the firstfruits, the pledge and foretaste, the down payment on our heritage], in anticipation of its full redemption and our acquiring [complete] possession of it—to the praise of His glory"*. This is amazing that God would even need an inheritance because He owns everything and yet here Moses clearly states that the Lord's portion is His people also 1 Peter 2:9 "But ye are a chosen generation, a royal priesthood, an holy nation, a peculiar people; that ye should shew forth the praises of him who hath called you out of darkness into his marvellous light". That we belong to God is an awesome thought. We are His own possession. He considers each of us to be His precious portion. This thought is too great to fully comprehend in this life! We belong to somebody. We have His "seal" on us, and more accurately within us in the presence of the Holy Spirit of God.

Power

This is incomparable, supernatural power to do things that we cannot do naturally. This is awesome and it is great. What a powerful God we serve. This same power was made available to Jesus—Acts 10:38 *"How God anointed Jesus of Nazareth with the Holy Ghost and with power: who went about doing good, and healing all that were oppressed of the devil; for God was with him"*. The power that is made available to us that believed and have intimate relationship with God comes first with receiving the Holy Spirit and the Holy Spirit makes the supernatural power available to us. The power of God through the Holy Spirit that can break evil yokes, destroy the works of darkness, power to live a Christ-like life, power to live above sin, temptations, lack, oppositions, oppressions, sickness, power to live a sin free life, power to be who God has destined you to be, power to have wealth, live in peace and power to attain what you are created on earth for. If we consider the example of Jesus Christ who was on the earth for 30 years as an ordinary man until the Holy Spirit came upon Him—Mat. 3:16-17 *"And Jesus, when he was baptized, went up straightway out of the water: and, lo, the heavens were opened unto him, and he saw the Spirit of God descending like a dove, and lighting* upon him:*17* *And lo a voice from heaven, saying, This is my beloved Son, in whom I am well pleased"*. It was when Jesus received the Holy Spirit that is when the power from God was made available to Him, power to boldly preach the Word of God, power to rebuke the devil, power to face and overcome temptations and trials, power to pray, to be obedient, love, heal, to do miracles, power to live above flesh and power to do all things that is in line with His Father's will. In fact, this great power made Him a celebrity; He was well known all over the cities, and was famous—Luke 4:14 *"And Jesus returned in the power of the Spirit into Galilee: and there went out a fame of him through all the region round about"*. If you are willing to know God personally and have Him transform your life, you too will receive the Holy Spirit and with supernatural powers that will make you a pacesetter like Jesus and you will be "Light of the world. A city set on a hill that cannot be hidden —Mat. 5:14". Amen.

Furthermore, one of the key manifestations of the Holy Spirit is "POWER". In Acts 1:8 *"But you shall receive power when the Holy Spirit has come upon you; and you shall be witnesses to Me in Jerusalem, and in all Judea and Samaria, and to the end of the earth"*. The gift of the Holy Spirit is the power from on high as Jesus told His disciples—Luke 4:18-19 (AMP) *"The Spirit of the Lord [is] upon Me, because He has anointed Me [the Anointed One, the Messiah] to preach the good news (the Gospel) to the poor; He has sent Me to announce release to the captives and recovery of sight to the blind, to send forth as delivered those who are oppressed [who are downtrodden, bruised, crushed, and broken down by calamity], ¹⁹ To proclaim the accepted and acceptable year of the Lord [the day [l]when salvation and the free favors of God profusely abound]"*. The scripture above explains that the Spirit of the Lord is the spirit of power. The question is what can the power that you now have through the Holy Spirit do?

- **To subdue the enemy:**—Ps. 110: 1-3 *"The Lord (God) says to my Lord (the Messiah), Sit at My right hand, until I make Your adversaries Your footstool. ² The Lord will send forth from Zion the scepter of Your strength; rule, then, in the midst of Your foes. ³ Your people will offer themselves willingly in the day of Your power, in the beauty of holiness and in holy array out of the womb of the morning; to You [will spring forth] Your young men, who are as the dew"*. This power is to subdue the enemy, to take authority over powers of darkness, to stop the attacks and Satan from oppressing or opposing you that "the devil is no longer in charge". The power you have now will enable you to rule over sicknesses, failures, rule over your enemies, and your progress can no longer be impeded anymore nor your breakthroughs be blocked. That is the essence of power. So, what you carry inside of you is power that can tread upon serpents and scorpions and is above all the power of the enemy (Luke 10:19).

The power of God will make way for you and you will never remain the same again. The summary list below explicates more on the blessing that God has in store for you.

- Access to God: Eph. 3:12
- Adoption into God's Family: John 1:12-13; Gal. 3:26
- Christ's Indwelling: Eph. 3:16-17
- Full of God's Peace: John 16:33
- God's Blessing: Ps. 40:4; Ps. 84:12; Prov. 16:20; Prov. 28:25; Isa. 57:13; Jer. 17:7-8

- God's Empowering: Matt. 17:20; Matt. 21:21-22; John 14:12-14

- God's Guidance: Ps. 143:8; Prov. 3:5-6; John 12:36; John 12:46

- God's Intercession: John 17:20

- God's Protection: Ps. 36:7; Ps. 57:1; Ps. 62:8; Ps. 91:2; Ps. 115:9-11; Prov. 29:25

- God's Indwelling: 1 John 4:15

- God's Love: Ps. 32:10; John 16:27

- God's Grace: Rom. 5:1-2

- Joy: John 15:11; 17:13 Acts 16:34; Rom. 15:13; 1 Pet. 1:8-9

- Forgiveness of Sin: Acts 10:42-43; Acts 13:38-39; Rom. 3:25

- Peace: John 14:1; Rom. 15:13

- The Spirit's Indwelling: John 7:38-39; John 14:16-17; Romans 8:9; Gal. 3:13-14; Eph. 1:13-14

- Spiritual Salvation: Isa. 28:16; John 3:14-18; John 3:36; John 6:35, 40, 47; John 11:25-26; John 20:31; Acts 16:31; Rom. 10:8-11; Eph. 2:8; 2 Thess. 2:13; 1 Tim. 1:16; 1 Tim. 6:12; 2 Tim. 3:15; Heb. 4:2-3; Heb. 10:39; 1 Pet. 1:3-5, 9; 1 John 5:13

These and many more are the benefits of knowing God personally and having a daily relationship with God through meditation on the Word of God, being the doer of the word (Josh. 1:8, James 1:22, 25), through prayers (Mark 1:35, Luke 6:12, Jer. 29:13), waiting on God (Isa. 40:31). The next chapter explains in details pursuit and principles to received divine guidance from God.

CHAPTER EIGHT

God's Guidance

You will also realise that the most important thing in life is '**purpose**'. God is more concerned about His purpose for your life. Myles Munroe explained that "*The most tragic thing in life is not death but it is a life without a purpose*—being in life without knowing why?" Why are you in this world? What is your reason for existence? What are you meant to be doing?—**Myles Munroe**

One of the greatest tragedies of life is to lack the knowledge of where you are going as well as not knowing how to get there —**Dr. David Oyedepo**

We are all faced with decisions and crossroads at one point or another in our lives. Some decisions are simple and some are very complex. Whatever the decision, all our decisions have consequences. Every decision and step you take now will either take you forward or backward. Actually, one of the greatest tragedies that can happen to a person is the lack of any idea where he or she is going and how to get there as many have rushed into certain offers, opportunities, or jobs, only to discover that they were traps in disguise. People have been deceived by the glamour of certain Job offers, business offers, Promising relationships, and have come to realise that not all that glitters is gold and that is why this book is timely.

We need God's directions because often, the decisions we make in life are based on our own assessment, which may not be absolutely correct. Everything may seem right and appear satisfactory to the human eye, but at the end of it is frustration, stagnation and untimely death—**Proverbs 14:12** *"¹²There is a way which seems right to a man and appears straight before him, but at the end of it is the way of death"*.

Your decision may be over a relationship, buying property, buying a car, leaving or staying at a job, moving to another location, taking a vacation, leaving or staying at a church, renting an apartment, starting a business, finding a job, doing charity work, running for a charity and many more. You may be thinking, does this mean I cannot simply sit down and plan what I want to do and pursue it? What is all this about directions? Remember Isaiah 55:8 *"For My thoughts are not your thoughts, neither are your ways My ways, says the Lord"*. Please understand that you are limited as a human being and that is why you will always need God's divine guidance.

How nice will it be, if the Lord Himself will give us the directions to proceed in our life? That is what exactly the Lord wants to do for His children. In the modern days that we live in, we have so many advanced technologies to give us directions when we want to get somewhere. The Bible talks about divine direction in the scriptures. God has a road map for each and every one of us. God knows exactly where to take us. He knows the minute details of our life. He has the blue print for our whole life already. We do not have to ask him to put a new plan for our lives. All we have to do it just fit in His plans for our lives. The Word of God declares in Jeremiah 29:11 "For I know the thoughts that I think toward you, says the Lord, thoughts of peace and not of evil, to give you a future and a hope". To get to the bigger picture, our God goes step by step. Though He knows the end from the beginning, He does not tell you the destination right away. All He wants to tell you is one step at a time. And the Lord God Almighty orders each step—Ps. 37:23 "The steps of a *good* man are ordered by the LORD, And He delights in his way".

If you go to a restaurant to eat, you will order as much as you can eat, likewise as a child of God and as stated in Ps. 37:23, God will only provide you with the "**order**" of what you can handle at every stage of your life. The word that is mentioned in the Bible is "**ordered**" just like the way you order your food in a restaurant. You order as much as you can eat. In the same way, God orders our steps and the steps that we are able to take. God's word says, "He orders every step". *"The steps of a good man are ordered by the Lord, and He delights in his way"* (Ps 37:23).

Have you noticed the way we plan things in our life? Most of them do not happen at all. Sometime people are concerned about things that may not even come to pass. I remember a story of a friend who had some plans in his head and decided to implement the plans. He made his decisions that he knew how he can raise money for needy and without praying about it, without any consultation or counsel from God or God's ministers. He decided to go about it in his own way as he had intelligent strategies and all plans are in place. He decided to prioritise his life by jogging daily mornings and evenings, most time missing Church services, ignore some of his roles and responsibilities in the local church and as the day to run the marathon approaches he was so excited and had done enough practice and ready for the day to come by. Guess what?

Few days to the marathon he collapsed at work and sustained injuries and the doctors recommends that he needed to rest for months. Friends, he could not participate in the marathon that he prepared for, planned for months, wasted time and efforts because he failed to allow God that created him to order his steps. Isa. 55:8 ""*For My thoughts are not your thoughts, Nor are your ways My ways," says the LORD*". 'God's ways, His plans and thoughts are different from ours. God has a road map for each and every one of us. God knows exactly where to take us. He knows the minute details of our life. He has the blue print for our whole life already. We do not have to ask Him to put a new plan for our lives. All we have to do is just fit in His plans for our lives. We need to make sure we are asking God for directions and aligning our plans with His plan so that we can eradicate mistakes, errors and so that we can live a life that is free of stress, frustrations, resentment, hatred, regrets, dejection, depression, disobedience, aggression, anger, rage, rebellion etc. Still, there are some who spend half of their time just worrying about things that are irrelevant? The Bible says, *"A man's heart plans his way, But the Lord directs his steps"* (Pro 16:9).

The key to unlocking God's direction is by acknowledging Him in all our ways. *"Trust in the Lord with all your heart, And lean not on your own understanding; In all your ways acknowledge Him and He shall direct your paths"* (Pro 3:5-6). Many think that God's paths are full of lack. That is not true. Just because you have not seen abundance does not means that God's paths are not abundant. The Bible says, *"You crown the year with Your goodness, And Your paths drip with abundance"* (Ps 65:11)

When we are in God's direction, we are heading towards abundance. It may not feel like it, it may not look like it. But the Word of God says God's path drip with abundance. Let not the devil talk you out of that word. Our God is not a God of lack. He is a God of abundance. His paths drip with abundance. All you want to be is in His path. God's word is final.

What is God's Plan for your life?

God has a plan for your life, a good plan actually. He said in Jeremiah 29:11 *"For I know the thoughts and plans that I have for you, says the Lord, thoughts and plans for welfare and peace and not for evil, to give you hope in your final outcome"*. God is a God of plan and purpose. Just as a manufacturer will not create a product without a set of goal in mind, without a handbook or brochure for its effective operation and maintenance, you are created to fulfill a definite purpose on earth. You are not created by accident and to be ignorant of your place in God's plan can lead to a life of toiling and frustrations. Paul in Acts 26:16 *"But rise and stand on your feet; for I have appeared to you for this purpose, to make you a minister and a witness both of the things which you have seen and of the things which I will yet reveal to you"*. He knew God's purpose for his life. His purpose is to be a minister and a witness for Christ. Likewise, Jeremiah 1:5 *"Before I formed you in the womb I knew you; Before you were born I sanctified you; I ordained you a prophet to the nations"*, Jesus also was sent for a purpose as emphasized in Luke 4:43 *"but He said to them," I must preach the kingdom of God to the other cities also, because for this purpose I have been sent"*. The truth is that God had a plan for your life before he even formed you in your mother's womb. He set you apart for a divine purpose on the earth even before you were born, just as the case with Paul, Jeremiah, and Jesus Christ.

How do I discover God's plan

Revelation of what you are created to do here on earth is called "**Vision**". Vision is disclosure of plan and purpose. Everyone is created to fulfill a purpose and the discovery of the reason for which you are created is also called "**Vision**". Divine vision is step by step revelation of where you are going or what you are meant to do on earth while directions is the steps you need to take to accomplished your vision. God revealed His purpose for creating Prophet Jeremiah "*Before I formed you in the womb I knew [and] approved of you [as My chosen instrument], and before you were born I separated and set you apart, consecrating you; [and] I appointed you as a prophet to the nations*"(Jer. 1:5).

He also had a purpose for Apostle Paul "*But arise and stand upon your feet; for I have appeared to you for this purpose, that I might appoint you to serve as [My] minister and to bear witness both to what you have seen of Me and to that in which*

I will appear to you, [17] [a]Choosing you out [selecting you for Myself] and [b]delivering you from among this [Jewish] people and the Gentiles to whom I am sending you—[18] To open their eyes that they may turn from darkness to light and from the power of Satan to God, so that they may thus receive forgiveness and release from their sins and a place and portion among those who are consecrated and purified by faith in Me".

Jesus too had a purpose why His Father sent Him to this earth in Luke 4:43 *"But He said to them, I must preach the good news (the Gospel) of the kingdom of God to the other cities [and towns] also, for I was sent for this [purpose]"* and likewise Luke 19:10 *"For the Son of Man came to seek and to save that which was lost".*

Jeremiah's purpose was to be a prophet, Paul to be a minister and Jesus to be a preacher, a restorer, to save and to establish the Kingdom of God here on earth. God has a purpose where He created you. Do you know the purpose yet? According to Bishop David Oyedepo, ***"Vision is knowing what you are here on earth for. It is a divine insight into God's plan for your life, and it is very important that you discover what it is, as it puts an end to a life of struggles".***

Divine Directions

When God reveals His plan and purpose to Moses *"And the Lord said, I have surely seen the affliction of My people who are in Egypt, and have heard their cry because of their taskmasters and oppressors; for I know their sorrows and sufferings and trials. ⁸ And I have come down to deliver them out of the hand and power of the Egyptians and to bring them up out of that land to a land good and large, a land flowing with milk and honey [a land of plenty]—to the place of the Canaanite, the Hittite, the Amorite, the Perizzite, the Hivite, and the Jebusite. ⁹ Now behold, the cry of the Israelites has come to Me, and I have also seen how the Egyptians oppress them. ¹⁰ Come now therefore, and I will send you to Pharaoh, that you may bring forth My people, the Israelites, out of Egypt"*—Exo.3:7-10. As Moses was called to be Israel's deliverer (that's God's purpose for his life), he insisted on how he can go about fulfilling the purpose of God in Egypt. God might have spoken to you also or reveal things to you about your career, future partner, your marriage, moving to another city, pursuing your academics, staying or leaving a job and much more. This is where "direction" is needed.

Moses asked God for details about the vision given to him and also asked for the "**how to**" as well in Exo. 3:11-16 "[11] And Moses said to God, [b]Who am I, that I should go to Pharaoh and bring the Israelites out of Egypt? [12] God said, I will surely be with you; and this shall be the sign to you that I have sent you: when you have brought the people out of Egypt, you shall serve God on this mountain [Horeb, or Sinai].[13] And Moses said to God, Behold, when I come to the Israelites and say to them, The God of your fathers has sent me to you, and they say to me, What is His name? What shall I say to them? [14] And God said to Moses, I AM WHO I AM *and* WHAT I AM, *and* I WILL BE WHAT I WILL BE; and He said, You shall say this to the Israelites: I AM has sent me to you! [15] God said also to Moses, This shall you say to the Israelites: The Lord, the God of your fathers, of Abraham, of Isaac, and of Jacob, has sent me to you! This is My [c]name forever, and by this name I am to be remembered to all generations. [16] Go, gather the elders of Israel together [the mature teachers and tribal leaders], and say to them, The Lord God of your fathers, the God of Abraham, of Isaac, and of Jacob, appeared to me, saying, I have surely visited you and seen that which is done to you in Egypt".

If Moses could ask God for details about the assignment given to him, and got directions as to how to go about it. Why will God not answer you or provide step by step details of the reason why He created you. If Paul the Apostle also obtain vision and directions from God on why he was created, why wouldn't you, if Jesus Christ the son of God (Our Saviour) has detailed step by step vision and directions from the Father, how much more you. This is why we need vision and directions from God. Vision is what shows you where you are to be (i.e shows you the Promised Land), while directions is the way to get to the Promised Land.

"Divine direction is a lifetime demand. You will never get to a point in life where you will no longer require direction. This is because life without direction is nothing but continuous frustration! Friends, understand that divine direction is required for every vision to succeed"

The reason why many are frustrated is because they celebrate vision without instruction. They have a go-ahead without approach. God is an orderly God. Every decision you make in life should be traceable to specific instructions received from

God, for instructions are the highways to distinction in life— Bishop David Oyedepo.

If you have received a vision regarding your marital life, your career, or a call to leadership or vision to join a ministry or business from God, then wait to receive the "how to" from God as well. Hab 2:3. It is only after you have done this that you can then set out in pursuit of the vision. Divine direction comes as instructions from God. Proverbs 8:33 *"Hear instruction and be wise, and do not refuse or neglect it".* The next chapter provides extensive ways to recognize God's directions.

CHAPTER NINE

How To Recognise God's Directions

There are several ways to receive God's directions. God knows exactly what direction He wants to lead you. He has even pre-planned the route to get you to your place of appointment. King David understood this clearly and said *"Show me Your ways, O Lord; teach me Your paths. 5 Guide me in Your truth and faithfulness and teach me, for You are the God of my salvation; for You [You only and altogether] do I wait [expectantly] all the day long"*-Ps. 25:3-4.

He knew that receiving directions from God will involve asking the creator Himself in prayers and allow Him to teach (instruct, impart knowledge, advice) as the only one who can direct to the right path (simply your destination or where God has promised you to be in life). These are ways to receive divine directions from God:

Prayer

Let's study the prayer of David, a man after God's own heart. David was a king but yet He had the time to pray to the Lord God Almighty to show him His ways and teach him His paths. *"Show me your ways, O Lord; teach me Your paths"* (Ps 25:4). Direct my steps by Your Word (Ps 119:136). Take God at His word when you pray. *I will instruct you and teach you in the way you should go; I will guide you with my eye* (Ps 32:8). When you talk to God in prayers that, *"Lord Jesus, I (Your Name) ask for your directions in my life today, teach me your paths, guide me on how to go about your directions".* I do not want to go in my own path or make my own decisions without you but take me through your ways, Lord. Exo. 33:13-14 *"Now therefore, I pray You, if I have found favor in Your sight, show me now Your way, that I may know You [progressively become more deeply and intimately acquainted with You, perceiving and recognizing and understanding more strongly and clearly] and that I may find favor in Your sight. And [Lord, do] consider that this nation is Your people.[14] And the Lord said, My Presence shall go with you, and I will give you rest".*

Word of God

God wants you to know His ways from His word and that is why King David said, *"Thy word is a lamp unto my feet, and a light unto my path"*—Ps. 119:105. After you have prayed, do not expect a prophet to come out, and put his hand on you give you to give a prophecy. That may not happen although to some, it may happen. That is not always the way God wants to work. Expect God to reveal things from His heart to yours. The word of God directs you on how to go about any assignment committed into your hands. If you are a Bible lover, you will never lack direction. In Luke 5:1-7, Peter and his men laboured through the night but caught nothing.

Later Jesus came on the scene and said to him, "Launch out into the deep for a catch." He gave them an instruction and when they obeyed, they pulled in a great catch. This suggests that instructions and directions from God is the gateway to achievements. If you follow God's instructions, you will not struggle in life. Peter was already tired and was washing and tiding up his net, struggled all through the night with no result, possibly fed up of their unsuccessful life, life of toiling, life of unproductivity, living from hand to mouth. But the moment they allow Jesus to direct their steps, obeyed His instructions and guidance—**His Word**, their lives were transformed and from being a mere fisherman to being a renowned fisherman. The whole region heard about their achievements, their success stories and how they made it in life.

Friends, divine direction comes through the word of God. 2 Tim 3:16, Joshua 1:8. Meditate on the word of God daily *"This Book of the Law shall not depart out of your mouth, but you shall meditate on it day and night, that you may observe and do according to all that is written in it. For then you shall make your way prosperous, and then you shall deal wisely and have good [b]success"*. There are benefits of meditating, analysing and applying the word of God daily in our lives also.

These are just overview of the benefits of the word of God.

- **Directs, Guides and gives illuminations: Psalm 119:105**
- **Reveals: James 1:22-25, Hebrews 4:12**
- **Protects: Ephesians 6:10-28, Psalm 119:9-11**
- **Feeds: Matthew 4:4**

- Grows: **John 17:17, 1 Peter 2:3**
- **Builds: Matthew 7:24-29**
- **Teaches: 2 Timothy 3:16**
- **Transforms: Romans 12:1-2**
- Breaks power of sin and corrects: **Ps. 119:11,** 2 Peter 1:3-4
- Builds your faith: **Rom. 10:17**
- Victory over Satan and Temptations: **Eph. 6:17, Mat. 4.**

Listen to the voice of the Holy Spirit

The most important thing that we need to understand is that we cannot hurry God into anything. The scriptures says in Isa. 40:31 *"But those who wait for the Lord [who expect, look for, and hope in Him] shall change and renew their strength and power; they shall lift their wings and mount up [close to God] as eagles [mount up to the sun]; they shall run and not be weary, they shall walk and not faint or become tired"*. Waiting upon the Lord is very important in our spiritual walk. The Holy Spirit talks in a still, small voice right in your heart. He loves to talk to us. When our heart is in the right place, we are sure we will hear Him speak to us. Isaiah 30:21 says, 'Your ears shall hear a word behind you, saying, *"This is the way, walk in it." Whenever you turn to the right hand Or whenever you turn to the left".* Jesus said in John 10:27 says, *"My sheep hear My voice, and I know them, and they follow Me".*

*"God also gives directions through the voice of the Holy Spirit. The voice of the Holy Spirit, which is the voice of God, is a majestic voice (Ps 29). Is London in the Bible or Canada? No. So, how do you know when you are to go to London or Canada? How would you know when you are to go there? It is by the voice of the Spirit. If someone comes to you in search for job in your company, how would you know if he is the right person to employ? It is by the voice of the Spirit, which many of us know as the witness of the Spirit. I pray that your spiritual ears be popped open to hear Him. Amen. John 16:13. Paying attention to the voice of the Spirit is a great step to achieving success in life—Isaiah 30:21. Being sincere in whatever you are doing is not enough to guarantee your success, because you can be sincerely wrong and that is why you must know what God's will is—Eph.5:17"—***Bishop David Oyedepo**.

We need to fine tune our spiritual ears all the time so that we can hear Him. Let us walk in His ways all the days of our life. The next chapter provides in-depth requirements of obtaining divine directions from God.

CHAPTER TEN

Requirements of Getting Divine Directions

It is very important to realize that not everyone is entitled to the instructions, leading, guidance and directions of God. It is only for those who are willing to be His disciples as well as His sheep. Jesus explicated this in detail in John 10:25-28 "*25 Jesus answered them, I have told you so, yet you do not believe Me [you do not trust Me and rely on Me]. The very works that I do by the power of My Father and in My Father's name bear witness concerning Me [they are My credentials and evidence in support of Me]. 26 But you do not believe and trust and rely on Me because you do not belong to My fold [you are no sheep of Mine]. 27 The sheep that are My own hear and are listening to My voice; and I know them, and they follow Me. 28 And I give them eternal life, and they shall never lose it or perish throughout the ages. [To all eternity they shall never by any means be destroyed.] And no one is able to snatch them out of My hand—John 10:25-28*". This means that we must meet God's conditions in order to have access to His divine directions.

Believe in Him

The first prerequisite is that you must believe in Christ, trust and rely on Him by grace through faith *"For it is by free grace (God's unmerited favor) that you are saved ([c] delivered from judgment and made partakers of Christ's salvation) through [your] faith. And this [salvation] is not of yourselves [of your own doing, it came not through your own striving], but it is the gift of God;⁹ Not because of works [not the fulfilment of the Law's demands], lest any man should boast. [It is not the result of what anyone can possibly do, so no one can pride himself in it or take glory to himself"]—*Eph. 2:8-9. Salvation is made available to us freely by God's unmerited favour 'GRACE' through 'FAITH'. It is free and not because we worked for it or because we are righteous, even while we were yet sinners Christ died for us. Romans 5:8.

The only medium that we have to receive Christ freely is through faith. And this means believing that God exists and trusting Him with our lives *"But without faith it is impossible to please and be satisfactory to Him. For whoever would come near to God must [necessarily] believe that God exists and that He is the rewarder of those who earnestly and diligently seek Him [out]—Heb. 11:6"*. You must believe that God exists and He is the only one that you can rely on and will never fail. So, for God to be committed to leading and directing you, you must first believe in Him, receive Him as your personal Lord and saviour and be His Child *"Jesus answered him, I assure you, most solemnly I tell you, that unless a person is born again (anew, from above), he cannot ever see (know, be acquainted with, and experience) the kingdom of God, . . . Jesus answered, I assure you, most solemnly I tell you, unless a man is born of water and [[a]even] the Spirit, he cannot [ever] enter the kingdom of God—John 3:3, 5"*. You need to be born again—being born of the Spirit, living a life that is led by the spirit of God. Walk by the Spirit so that you will not fulfil the lust of the flesh . . . Gal. 5:16. When you accept Jesus as your personal Lord and Saviour, this is first to receiving divine directions. God is now committed to leading, guiding and directing you in all aspects of your life.

Obedience

After accepting to be part of the sheepfold (be part of the family of God), you need to be able to listen to and take instructions and obey them for you to be guided and be led by God "*26 But you do not believe and trust and rely on Me because you do not belong to My fold [you are no sheep of Mine]. 27 The sheep that are My own hear and are listening to My voice; and I know them, and they follow Me. 28 And I give them eternal life, and they shall never lose it or perish throughout the ages. [To all eternity they shall never by any means be destroyed.] And no one is able to snatch them out of My hand—John 10:26-28"*. Being obedient to God and to His instructions must be in place in your life before God can show you His ways. You must be willing to pay attention to details, ready to obey God at all times in all situations no matter your circumstances and whatever what you are passing through. Obedience is one of the keys to gaining access to divine directions. Jesus also confirms this "*15 If you [really] love Me, you will keep (obey) My commands—John 14:15"*. Obedience is God's commands and also His expectations for us to be guided by Him—**Ephesians 6:1-3** *"Children, obey your parents in the Lord, for this is right. "Honor your father and mother" (this is the first commandment with a promise), "that it may go well with you and that you may live long in the land"*.

Colossians 3:22 *"Slaves, obey in everything those who are your earthly masters, not by way of eye-service, as people-pleasers, but with sincerity of heart, fearing the Lord".*

Hebrews 13:17 (KJV) *"Obey them that have the rule over you, and submit yourselves: for they watch for your souls, as they that must give account, that they may do it with joy, and not with grief: for that is unprofitable for you".*

Commitment

You need to be God's disciple to be directed by Him, Jesus said *"Believe and trust and rely on Me because you do not belong to My fold [you are no sheep of Mine]. ²⁷ The sheep that are My own hear and are listening to My voice; and I know them, and they follow Me"* John 10:27. Divine direction is not for those who are not willing to follow or be committed to Him. When you commit yourself to God, you commit to obey Him and with commitment, comes responsibility. You will realise that commitment is a two-edged sword. Jesus reveals our commitment as His disciples. *"If anyone comes to Me and does not hate his father and mother, wife and children, brothers and sisters, yes, and his own life also, he cannot be My disciple. And whoever does not bear his cross and come after Me cannot be My disciple"* (<u>Luke 14:26-27</u>).

We must love Jesus above everything and everyone on earth and we must put Him first. Jesus says, *"If anyone desires to come after Me, let him deny himself, and take up his cross, and follow Me. For whoever desires to save his life will lose it, and whoever loses his life for My sake will find it. For what is a man profited if he gains the whole world, and loses his own soul? Or what will a man give in exchange for his soul"* <u>Matt. 16:24-26</u>. He requires a total, complete, sacrificial commitment from people who desire to be His disciples. But at the same time, Jesus has shown us the way to salvation by living the committed life He requires of us. Jesus is therefore a sympathetic High Priest <u>Heb. 4:14-16</u>, leaving us an example of total commitment to God, *"Who committed no sin, nor was guile found in His mouth; who, when He was reviled, did not revile in turn; when He suffered, He did not threaten, but committed Himself to Him who judges righteously"* <u>1 Pet. 2:22-23</u>.

Thus, Jesus demonstrated commitment. He committed Himself to God by living righteously, and by suffering in order to bear our sins upon the cross and by His stripes we've been healed <u>1 Pet. 2:24</u>. If you are committed to God, you will be guaranteed divine directions.

Praise and Worship

Praise and worship must be part and parcel of your life if you want to gain access to divine directions from God. Paul and Silas needed help, solutions, directions and deliverance for their lives in Acts 16:22-26 "*²² The crowd [also] joined in the attack upon them, and the rulers tore the clothes off of them and commanded that they be beaten with rods. ²³ And when they had struck them with many blows, they threw them into prison, charging the jailer to keep them safely. ²⁴ He, having received [so strict a] charge, put them into the inner prison (the dungeon) and fastened their feet in the stocks. ²⁵ But about midnight, as Paul and Silas were praying and singing hymns of praise to God, and the [other] prisoners were listening to them, ²⁶ Suddenly there was a great earthquake, so that the very foundations of the prison were shaken; and at once all the doors were opened and everyone's shackles were unfastened*".
As God inhabits the praise of His people (Ps. 22:3), praise and worship connects you to God's throne of grace and that releases the divine miracles, deliverances, healing and even divine direction is guaranteed in His presence.

CHAPTER ELEVEN

Fulfilling Your Purpose On Earth (Practical Ways)

Jer. 1:4-5

⁴ Then the word of the Lord came to me [Jeremiah], saying,
⁵ Before I formed you in the womb I knew [and] approved
of you [as My chosen instrument], and before you were
born I separated *and* set you apart, consecrating you; [and]
I appointed you as a prophet to the nations.

Eccl. 3:12-13

*¹² I know that there is no good in them, but for a man to
rejoice, and to do good in his life.*

*¹³ And also that every man should eat and drink, and enjoy the
good of all his labour, it is the gift of God.*

Enjoyment is determined by what you love, what
you are satisfied with or have pleasure in. Jeremiah's
purpose of existence has been determined before he was
born and that suggest that before all of us were born, God

has pre-determine our purpose. He knew why He created us, why we are located where we are and why we are who we are. In Eccl. 3:13, we discovered that the enjoyment of whatever we found ourselves satisfied with is a clue to God's purpose for our lives. Joy in your heart concerning your job, location, church, work places, friends, marital life, career, travelling and much more is determined by what you are passionate about.

So, what do you love doing, what comes to you naturally, what do you like doing if distance is not an issue, what do you do best and do not need anyone to teach you but comes without strife? What you love doing will be a clue to God's given purpose in your life. Studying the life of Moses (Exo. 3:1); he was leading sheep, he loves his job, was dedicated to it. Therefore, his leadership skills to lead, direct and defend are clues to what God wanted to use him and what God has created him for—an humble leader—to lead and deliver the Israelites from their bondages. Paul loves public prosecutions, speaking and teaching as a renowned prosecutor and this was a clue to understanding God's purpose for his life. When he gave his life to Christ, Paul became a public speaker for Christ—a minister actually. Here are some biblical examples of how we can discover God's purpose for our lives and how God discovers our potentials:

Moses: Exo. 2: 11-14: "[11] One day, after Moses was grown, it happened that he went out to his brethren and looked at their burdens; and he saw an Egyptian beating a Hebrew, one of [Moses'] brethren. [12] He looked this way and that way, and when he saw no one, he killed the Egyptian and hid him in the sand.[13] He went out the second day and saw two Hebrew men quarreling *and* fighting; and he said to the unjust aggressor, Why are you striking your comrade? [14] And the man said, Who made you a prince and a judge over us? Do you intend to kill me as you killed the Egyptian? Then Moses was afraid and thought, Surely this thing is known."

You can deduce from the scripture above that Moses does not like cheating, does not like to be discriminated upon, or detest denial of right of individuals, he loves to defend people's rights, protect people interest, he loves to defend people, love helping people as much as it is within his capacity to do, especially when it is not at the expense of losing their privileges. So, at some stage in his life (40 years of age) he saw his citizen being beaten, he decided to defend his country mate's (a Hebrew) right. Despite living in the king's palace where he grew up with the Egyptians, he decided to defend his country mate; although he was extreme in his judgment and this led to the death of the Egyptian man. However, realizing his passion to always stand for truth and defend people's interest provided a clue to his purpose, calling, talent, and career in life. In all that had happened, God did not give up on Moses. He just used the circumstances to continue Moses' training, despite the mistakes made by Moses.

Likewise, on a separate occasion, Moses was sitting by a well and some young women came with a flock of sheep. They went to draw water from the well to water the sheep, but the other shepherds chased them away. Moses came to help them and drew water for all the sheep. The women thanked him and told their father Jethro how they were able to water the sheep so quickly. Their father told them to bring the man to their house. Moses was invited to stay with their family and later married the man's daughter Zipporah. Jethro was a priest in the land of Midian. Moses began to take care of Jethro's flock of sheep. He led them to the west side of the wilderness, to a mountain called Horeb, the "mountain of God." It is so evident that Moses has passion to help people, lead, defend and stand for the rights of individual leading to his purpose on earth—*A Servant of God, a Leader and Priest of God—assigned to deliver, defend and lead* the Israelites from their oppression and bondage in Egypt unto the promised land. Exo. 3:7-15. What a great career!

7 And the Lord said, I have surely seen the affliction of My people who are in Egypt, and have heard their cry because of their taskmasters and oppressors; for I know their sorrows and sufferings andtrials.

8 And I have come down to deliver them out of the hand and power of the Egyptians and to bring them up out of that land to a land good and large, a land flowing with milk and honey [a land of plenty]—to the place of the Canaanite, the Hittite, the Amorite, the Perizzite, the Hivite, and the Jebusite.

9 Now behold, the cry of the Israelites has come to Me, and I have also seen how the Egyptians oppress them.

10 Come now therefore, and I will send you to Pharaoh, that you may bring forth My people, the Israelites, out of Egypt.

11 And Moses said to God, [b]Who am I, that I should go to Pharaoh and bring the Israelites out of Egypt?

12 God said, I will surely be with you; and this shall be the sign to you that I have sent you: when you have brought the people out of Egypt, you shall serve God on this mountain [Horeb, or Sinai].

13 And Moses said to God, Behold, when I come to the Israelites and say to them, The God of your fathers has sent me to you, and they say to me, What is His name? What shall I say to them?

14 And God said to Moses, I AM WHO I AM and WHAT I AM, and I WILL BE WHAT I WILL BE; and He said, You shall say this to the Israelites: I AM has sent me to you!

15 God said also to Moses, This shall you say to the Israelites: The Lord, the God of your fathers, of Abraham, of Isaac, and of Jacob, has sent me to you! This is My [c]name forever, and by this name I am to be remembered to all generations.

So, what about you? What are you passionate about and what do you enjoy doing best? What makes you happy every day of your life? Why not discover that first before making decisions or embarking on any assignment or before making a lifelong commitment to something or project?

You might have gone through a lot or thought many years have passed by and that they are all a waste. What do you expect Moses to say, at 40 years of age, he was just an ordinary shepherd leading flocks of sheep but when he got to understand God's purpose, calling upon his life, he obeyed God. At 80 years, Moses started his original career as destined by God as a "DELIVERER". Exo. 7:1-7 "*7 So the Lord said to Moses: "See, I have made you as God to Pharaoh, and Aaron your brother shall be your prophet. ² You shall speak all that I command you. And Aaron your brother shall tell Pharaoh to send the children of Israel out of his land. ³ And I will harden Pharaoh's heart, and multiply My signs and My wonders in the land of Egypt. ⁴ But Pharaoh will not heed you, so that I may lay My hand on Egypt and bring My armies and My people, the children of Israel, out of the land of Egypt by great judgments. ⁵ And the Egyptians shall know that I am the Lord, when I stretch out My hand on Egypt and bring out the children of Israel from among them." ⁶ Then Moses and Aaron did so; just as the Lord commanded them, so they did. ⁷ And Moses was eighty years old and Aaron eighty-three years old when they spoke to Pharaoh."* Moses was 80 years of age when he met Pharaoh again now on a real business fulfilling his purpose in life as a deliverer of the children of Israelites and he lived 40 years more. What an incredible life. Age is not a limitation to fulfilling God's purpose for your life. It is never too late to be innovative, creative and to have the successful life you hope for or dream of. Your success is not in the hand of the government, economy or people around you. The Psalmist says *"¹⁵ my times be in thine hands. Deliver thou me from the hands of mine enemies; and from them that pursue me. (my life is in thy hands. Rescue thou me from the power of my enemies; and from those who persecute me.)."*

What about David? What are the clues to the fulfillment of his purpose in life? 1 Sam. 17:23-38

²³ As they talked, behold, Goliath, the champion, the Philistine of Gath, came forth from the Philistine ranks and spoke the same words as before, and David heard him.

²⁴ And all the men of Israel, when they saw the man, fled from him, terrified.

25 *And the Israelites said, Have you seen this man who has come out? Surely he has come out to defy Israel; and the man who kills him the king will enrich with great riches, and will give him his daughter and make his father's house free [from taxes and service] in Israel.*

26 *And David said to the men standing by him, What shall be done for the man who kills this Philistine and takes away the reproach from Israel? For who is this uncircumcised Philistine that he should defy the armies of the living God?*

27 *And the [men] told him, Thus shall it be done for the man who kills him.*

28 *Now Eliab his eldest brother heard what he said to the men; and Eliab's anger was kindled against David and he said, Why did you come here? With whom have you left those few sheep in the wilderness? I know your presumption and evilness of heart; for you came down that you might see the battle.*

29 *And David said, What have I done now? Was it not a harmless question?*

30 And David turned away from Eliab to another and he asked the same question, and again the men gave him the same answer.

31 When David's words were heard, they were repeated to Saul, and he sent for him.

32 David said to Saul, Let no man's heart fail because of this Philistine; your servant will go out and fight with him.

33 And Saul said to David, You are not able to go to fight against this Philistine. You are only an adolescent, and he has been a warrior from his youth.

34 And David said to Saul, Your servant kept his father's sheep. And when there came a lion or again a bear and took a lamb out of the flock,

35 I went out after it and smote it and delivered the lamb out of its mouth; and when it arose against me, I caught it by its beard and smote it and killed it.

36 Your servant killed both the lion and the bear; and this uncircumcised Philistine shall be like one of them, for he has defied the armies of the living God!

37 David said, The Lord Who delivered me out of the paw of the lion and out of the paw of the bear, He will deliver me out of the hand of this Philistine. And Saul said to David, Go, and the Lord be with you!

38 Then Saul clothed David with his armor; he put a bronze helmet on his head and clothed him with a coat of mail.

David's passion to protect his father's sheep, his determination, courage to fight a lion and a bear which means being able to defend his right, and domain and being able to protect his sheep from attacks and able to prevent them from all risks and vulnerabilities. His passion to defend and stand for God and be against defilement was a clue to his purpose in life. Fighting for justice, to defend and protect as elucidated when he defended the sheep from lion and bear; this was David's passion and this led to discovering God's purpose for his life.

He defeated Goliath and as we know the rest of the story, he became the King of Israel and reigned for 40 years—2 Sam. 5:4-5 *"4 David was thirty years old when he began to reign, and he reigned forty years. 5 In Hebron he reigned over Judah seven years and six months: and in*

Jerusalem he reigned thirty and three years over all Israel and Judah. "Though he discovered his purpose early (30 years of age) and God honored that and his career lasted 40 years—a fulfilled person.

Even at 12 years of age, Jesus had a passion for ministry, teaching, preaching, liked to engage in intelligent and mature discussions as explained in Luke 2:41-52 *"41 His parents went to Jerusalem every year at the Feast of the Passover. 42 And when He was twelve years old, they went up to Jerusalem according to the custom of the feast. 43 When they had finished the days, as they returned, the Boy Jesus lingered behind in Jerusalem. And Joseph and His mother[l]did not know it; 44 but supposing Him to have been in the company, they went a day's journey, and sought Him among their relatives and acquaintances. 45 So when they did not find Him, they returned to Jerusalem, seeking Him. 46 Now so it was that after three days they found Him in the temple, sitting in the midst of the teachers, both listening to them and asking them questions. 47 And all who heard Him were astonished at His understanding and answers. 48 So when they saw Him, they were amazed; and His mother said to Him, "Son, why have You done this to us? Look, Your father and I have sought You anxiously."*

49 And He said to them, "Why did you seek Me? Did you not know that I must be about My Father's business?" 50 But they did not understand the statement which He spoke to them.

Jesus Advances in Wisdom and Favor

51 Then He went down with them and came to Nazareth, and was subject to them, but His mother kept all these things in her heart. 52 And Jesus increased in wisdom and stature, and in favor with God and men.". Jesus knew His purpose of existence that it is about His father's business (verse 49), it is about obeying God, working for God, ministering to people, healing the sick, raising the dead, deliverance from powers of darkness, regaining the kingdom that was lost during the time of Adam and Eve to re-establish the Kingdom of God on earth; for all humanity to have freedom and fulfillment of life.

So, Jesus fulfilled his purpose on earth. Jesus was about thirty years old when he began his ministry." In <u>Luke 3:23</u> *"Now Jesus Himself began His ministry at about thirty years of age, being (as was supposed) the son of Joseph, the son of Heli.",* This scripture gives us the life symbol of Jesus. The four Gospels (Matthew, Mark, Luke, John) then go on to describe a three year ministry of Jesus. So we know Jesus died, rose and ascended into heaven at about age 33. And Mat. 3:13-17 *"13 Then Jesus came from Galilee to John at the Jordan to be baptized by him. 14 And John tried to prevent Him, saying, "I need to be baptized by You, and are You coming to me?" 15 But Jesus answered and said to him, "Permit it to be so now, for thus it is fitting for us to fulfil all righteousness." Then he allowed Him.*

16 When He had been baptized, Jesus came up immediately from the water; and behold, the heavens were opened to Him, and He[c] saw the Spirit of God descending like a dove and alighting upon Him. 17 And suddenly a voice came from heaven, saying, "This is My beloved Son, in whom I am well pleased."

Jesus was confirmed for His purpose in life and at age 30, He began the work of ministry. In Luke 4:43 *"43 but He said to them, "I must preach the kingdom of God to the other cities also, because for this purpose I have been sent." 44 And He was preaching in the synagogues of Galilee.* "Jesus' purpose was revealed, He knew why He came to the planet earth—to fulfil a purpose, to live a life that has meaning, life that is productive, fruitful and full of joy. Also His purpose was revealed in details:

- **To destroy the works of the devil.**
- 1 John 3:8, *"He who sins is of the devil, for the devil has sinned from the beginning. For this purpose the Son of God was manifested, that He might destroy the works of the devil."*
- **Jesus Christ came into the world to save sinners.**
  1 Timothy 1:15, *"This is a faithful saying, and worthy of all acceptation, that Christ Jesus came into the world to save sinners; of whom I am chief."*
- **Came into the world to call sinners to repentance.**
- Mark 2:17, *"When Jesus heard it, he saith unto them, They that are whole have no need of the physician, but they that are sick: I came not to call the righteous, but sinners to repentance."*
- **Came into the world to seek and save the lost.**
- Luke 19:10, *"For the Son of man is come to seek and to save that which was lost."*
- **To demonstrate the true purpose of life and give Himself a ransom.**

- Matthew 20:28, *"Even as the Son of man came not to be ministered unto, but to minister, and to give his life a ransom for many."*
- **Jesus Christ came into the world to be a King and bear witness to the truth.**
- John 18:37, *"Pilate therefore said unto him, Art thou a king then? Jesus answered, Thou sayest that I am a king. To this end was I born, and for this cause came I into the world, that I should bear witness unto the truth. Every one that is of the truth heareth my voice."*
- **Jesus Christ came into the world to do the Will of His Father.**
- John 6:38, *"For I came down from heaven, not to do mine own will, but the will of him that sent me."*
- **To be a Light in the world.**
- John 12:46, *"I am come a light into the world, that whosoever believeth on me should not abide in darkness."*
- **So that men might have the Abundant Life.**
- John 10:10, *"I am come that they might have life, and that they might have it more abundantly."*
- **To Judge the world.**

- John 9:39, *"And Jesus said, For judgment I am come into this world, that they which see not might see; and that they which see might be made blind."*
- **To Proclaim or preach the Good News about the Kingdom of God.**
- Mark 1:38, *"And he said unto them, Let us go into the next towns, that I may preach there also: for therefore came I forth."*
- **To die on the cross so that we can be saved**
- John 12:27, *"Now is my soul troubled; and what shall I say? Father, save me from this hour: but for this cause came I unto this hour."*
- **To fulfil the law.**
- Matthew 5:17, *"Think not that I am come to destroy the law, or the prophets: I am not come to destroy, but to fulfil."*
- **To demonstrate God's Love.**
- 1 John 4:10, *"Herein is love, not that we loved God, but that he loved us, and sent his Son to be the propitiation for our sins."*
- **Because the Father sent Him.**
- John 20:21, *"Then said Jesus to them again, Peace be unto you: as my Father hath sent me, even so send I you."*

- The Father SENT Jesus to be the Propitiation (atonement) for our sins.
- 1 John 4:10, *"Herein is love, not that we loved God, but that he loved us, and sent his Son to be the propitiation for our sins."*
- The Father SENT Jesus and gave Jesus as the Saviour of the world.
- John 3:16-18, *"For God so loved the world, that he gave his only begotten Son, that whosoever believeth in him should not perish, but have everlasting life. For God sent not his Son into the world to condemn the world; but that the world through him might be saved. He that believeth on him is not condemned: but he that believeth not is condemned already, because he hath not believed in the name of the only begotten Son of God."*
- The Father SENT Jesus to bless us by turning us from our iniquities.
- Acts 3:26, *"Unto you first God, having raised up his Son Jesus, sent him to bless you, in turning away every one of you from his iniquities."*
- The Father SENT His Son to redeem us from the curse of the law.
- Galatians 4:4-5, *"But when the fulness of the time was come, God sent forth his Son, made of a woman, made*

under the law, To redeem them that were under the law, that we might receive the adoption of sons."

- God SENT His Son to make possible a new power in the hearts of men, the power to enable him to fulfil the righteousness of the law.

- Romans 8:3,4, *"For what the law could not do, in that it was weak through the flesh, God sending his own Son in the likeness of sinful flesh, and for sin, condemned sin in the flesh: That the righteousness of the law might be fulfilled in us, who walk not after the flesh, but after the Spirit."*

If Moses at age 80 years, King David at age 30 years and Jesus at about 30 years discovered and developed their passion which were clues to their purpose, calling and talent in life; since they were fulfilled and successful, why wouldn't you? If Moses at age 80 years only started his career and was fulfilled and God blessed his work to the extent that his career lasted 40 years, surely, it is not too late for you either. Stop being discouraged, hopes are not lost yet. Start to know God's purpose today and you are already in the process of enjoying a long lasting and fulfilled life. What they love most was a clue to the purpose of God in their lives. Fulfilling that purpose produced joy, happiness, long life, peace, abundance, riches, wealth, success, breakthroughs, Best Marital life, Excellent Career and Innovations, divine protections, divine favour in sight of God and men, divine wisdom, deliverances from powers of darkness, deliverances from curses and spell, and much more as God has good intentions and plans for your life. The fulfilled life you have been offered is not dependent on age, distance, location or government or the economy of your country, it solely depends on you discovering it and willing to get directions—"How to" from Him—Ps. 32:8.

CHAPTER TWELVE

Conclusion

This book is written to enlighten, educate, liberate and teach you about the season that you are in, to discover God's purpose for your life and to fulfil the glorious, joyous and abundance life He has destined for you. It is high time you start living a fulfilled, successful, and joyous life that God has destined for you. The abundant life you have been offered is not dependent on the government in power, economy, nation that you are in, neither is it dependent on the people that you know or level of your influences in authority but completely depends on God—the creator of the heaven and the earth. He is the manufacturer of our lives, we are the products and He gave us a manual—The word of God (Bible) to be read and understood for us to discover His purpose for our lives and to show us the secrets of fulfilment and success in life. Please read this book again and discover the practical ways to living a purpose driven life, innovative life as destined by God.

Realizing that discovering your 'purpose' is the most important thing in life could be something you have never expected. Living a purpose driven life will eradicate life of toiling, struggling, trial and error, untimely death. Purpose guarantees our reasons for existence. Reading through this book has provided an enlightened and expository experience that God is more concerned about His purpose for your life. In Prov. 19:21—*"many plans are in a man's mind, but it is the Lord's purpose for him that will stand"*. God wants us to align our plan with His plan. He wants us to submit our ideas, intentions, creativities, thoughts and align them with His purpose—His original reason why we are created. If the plans or thoughts or intentions or ideas are in line, then God's plan for our life will stand. Purpose is more important to God and His desires are for us to discover them and live a purpose driven life.

Purpose is the original intention of God for you, his original reason why He created you, original reason for your existence on earth. Discovering this is good news.